POETS' COF
FOREIGN
WRITERS, POETS & ARTI

A GUIDE TO LITERARY GRAVES IN MILITARY CEMETERIES
COMPILED BY LUCY LONDON

Front Cover Photos:
Cabaret Rouge British Cemetery (Commonwealth War Graves Commission)
Edward Thomas, Isaac Rosenberg, Wilfred Owen, Rupert Brooke.

Back Cover Photos:
Alan Seeger (American), Alfred Lichtenstein (German), Guillaume Apollinaire (French), Ewart Alan Mackintosh (British), John McCrae (Canadian).

Thiepval Memorial, The Somme, France - Caterpillar Valley Cemetery, Longueval, France - Menin Gate Memorial, Ypres, Belgium.

Interesting Books...
...Fascinating Subjects!

POSH UP NORTH
Publishing

www.poshupnorth.com

Published in Great Britain in April 2016 by
Posh Up North Publishing
2 Beckenham Road, New Brighton CH45 2NZ

British Library cataloguing in publication data.
A catalogue record for this book is available from the British Library

ISBN: 978-1-909643-08-6

CONTENTS

ACKNOWLEDGEMENTS

My thanks, as always, to Paul Breeze for his wonderful editing work turning my list of cemeteries where WW1 poets are buried into a book.

To Stephen Cribari of Minnesota for inspiring this book

And thank you to the following for their fantastic help with my commemorative project:

Johan R. Ryheul who is researching German WW1 Cemeteries - https://germancemeteriesofthegreatwarinbelgium.wordpress.com/

Timo Gälzer, Jurgen Verhulst and Maria Coates of the Facebook Group Cemeteries and Memorials of the Great War: https://www.facebook.com/groups/1609379815967794/

All my WW1 research is in loving memory of my Grandfather, who was an Old Contemptible who survived the war, and of my two Great Uncles – one of whom was killed at Arras on 9th April 1917 and the other, who was gassed and invalided home, who died aboard his Thames Barge after taking supplies to Dunkirk on 8th November 1918.

For Jimmy and David

INTRODUCTION
by Lucy London

The idea for this book about where to find the graves of poets killed during the First World War, came from Paul Breeze, who edits all my research so wonderfully well.

A friend of ours asked for advice regarding visiting the graves of some of the poets killed during the First World War, so I sent him the list I have been compiling since 2016. Paul suggested it might be easier if the information was in book form.

This is very much an on-going project. I only began researching forgotten poets of WW1 in 2016 for an exhibition of those involved in The Somme Offensive. For this particular section of the project, I need to go back and find those who were killed during 1914 and 1915.

I am currently researching the poets of 1918 for an exhibition in the autumn of 2018. For details of this self--funded commemorative WW1 exhibition project, please see my weblogs – another of Paul's amazing ideas:

Lucy London, August 2018
Email: info@femalewarpoets.com

www.fascinatingfactsofww1.blogspot.co.uk
www.inspirationalwomenofww1.blogspot.co.uk
www.femalewarpoets.blogspot.co.uk
www.forgottenpoetsofww1.blogspot.co.uk

Also on Facebook:
https://www.facebook.com/Inspirational-Women-of-World-War-One
https://www.facebook.com/femalepoetsofthefirstworldwar/
https://www.facebook.com/forgottenpoetsofww1/
https://www.facebook.com/fascinatingfactsofww1/

THE COMMONWEALTH WAR GRAVES COMMISSION

Lovingly tended, immaculate cemeteries with beautiful memorials – fitting tributes to our war dead – are something that we tend to take for granted these days. However, the concept of the War Graves Commission is owed to one man – Major General Sir Fabian Arthur Goulstone Ware, KCVO, KBE, CB, CMG (left).

During the First World War, Ware was too old to fight so instead he commanded a mobile Red Cross unit on the Western Front. He was appalled at the number of casualties and his unit began to record all the graves they came across. In 1915, this initiative was officially recognized by the British Government and was incorporated into the British Army as the "Graves Registration Commission".

Ware wanted his work to reflect the sacrifice of all the nations that helped Britain during WW1 and, with the encouragement of the Prince of Wales, who was himself a soldier on the Western Front during WW1, the Imperial War Graves Commission was set up with a Royal Charter.

The Commission demanded very high standards for its work. Three of the most famous architects of that time - Sir Edwin Lutyens, Sir Herbert Baker and Sir Reginald Blomfield - were chosen to design and build cemeteries and memorials. Rudyard Kipling was given the task, as its literary advisor, to advise the Commission with regard to inscriptions.

The Commonwealth War Graves Commission has an enormous task as there are official graves all over the world. If you want to find out details of where a family member killed during a war is commemorated, all you have to do is visit the Commission website - www.cwgc.org/

WAAC [Women's Army Auxiliary Corps] gardeners tending the graves of the war dead at Etaples.

The wooden crosses would later be replaced by white headstones.

Find more information about British and Commonwealth military cemeteries in the UK and abroad at:

CWGC
Commonwealth War Graves Commission

www.cwgc.org

For more information on American military cemeteries and monuments visit the website at:

www.abmc.gov

American Battle Monuments Commission
2300 Clarendon Boulevard, Arlington, VA 22201-3367, USA

The **German War Graves Commission** (*Volksbund Deutsche Kriegsgräberfürsorge* in German) is responsible for the maintenance and upkeep of German war graves in Europe and North Africa.

https://www.volksbund.de/en/volksbund.html

ARTILLERY WOOD MILITARY CEMETERY,
Near Boezinge, (8904 Ypres), Belgium

Boezinge is located north of the town of Ieper on the N369 road in the direction of Diksmuide. The Cemetery is located in the Poezelstraat, east of the village.

Ellis Humphrey EVANS (1887 – 1917)
Private, Royal Welch Fusiliers
Killed 31st July 1917 Pickem Ridge
Plot II. Row F. Grave 11.

(Pen-name Hedd Wyn)

Francis Edward LEDWIDGE, (1887 – 1917),
L/Corporal, Royal Inniskilling Fusiliers,
Killed 31st July 1917 Passchendaele
Plot II, Row B, Grave 5.
(The nearby spot where he was killed is marked by an Irish tricolour flag)

COXYDE MILITARY CEMETERY,
8670 Koksijde, West Flanders, BELGIUM

Coxyde Military Cemetery is located approximately 500 metres beyond the village of Koksijde on the N396 towards De Panne

Thomas Ernest HULME (1883 – 1917),
Honourable Artillery Company December 1914,
wounded 1915, killed 28th September 1917
Oost Duinkerke
Plot IV Row C Grave 2

Belgium

DICKEBUSCH NEW MILITARY CEMETERY
Kerkstraat, 8900 Ypres, BELGIUM

From Ieper town centre the Dikkebusseweg (N375), is reached via Elverdingsestraat, straight over a roundabout onto J.Capronstraat (for 30 metres), then left along M.Fochlaan.

Leslie George RUB, (1892 – 1917)
Private, Australian Pioneers
killed 23rd September 1917
Plot V, Row D, Grave No. 16

Robert William STERLING (1893-1915)
Lieutenant Royal Scots Fusiliers,
killed 23rd April 1915
Row D Grave 28

DUHALLOW A.D.S.* CEMETERY
Diksmuidseweg, 8900 Ieper, Belgium

The Cemetery is located on the Diksmuidseweg, N369 road, in the direction of Boezinge.

Thomas Ewart MITTON, (1897 – 1917),
Lieutenant, Royal Engineers,
killed 24th December 1917
Plot II Row E Grave 5

A.D.S. = Advance Dressing Station

HUY / HOEI: CIMITIERE COMMUNALE

Huy / Hoei is a small village in Belgium between Liège and Namur on the N66. Cemetery is also called La Sarte.

Gaston de RUYTER, (1895 – 1918)
Belgian poet and pilot in 11th Escadrille
Killed 7th October 1918 at Alveringhem.

Originally buried in de Panne Belgian Military Cemetery and later moved to family plot in Huy La Sarte

Belgium

LIJSSENTHOEK MILITARY CEMETERY
Boescheepseweg 35A, 8970 Poperinge, West-Vlaanderen

Lijssenthoek Military Cemetery is located 12 Kms west of Ieper town centre, on the Boescheepseweg, a road leading from the N308 connecting Ieper to Poperinge.

Leonard Comer WALL, (1897 – 1917),

Lieut, 1st West Lancs Bde of Royal Field Artillery. Killed at Ypres, 9th June 1917

(Note: his horse Blackie is buried at Hunts Cross RSPCA Centre, Liverpool)

Plot XIII Row B Grave 10

Please Also Visit:
SPINDLER, Staff Nurse, NELLIE.
44th Casualty Clearing Station, Queen Alexandra's Imperial Military Nursing Service.

Killed in action, 21 August 1917. Age 26.

One of only two female casualties of the Great War buried in Belgium.

Plot XVI Row A Grave 3

Belgium

MENDINGHEM MILITARY CEMETERY, 8972 Poperinge, Belgium

Mendinghem Military Cemetery is located 17 Kms north-west of Ieper town centre on the N308 connecting Ieper to Poperinge.

Arthur Hugh SIDGWICK (1882 – 1917),

Captain, Royal Garrison Artillery,
Killed 17th September 1917, near Ypres

(Younger brother of Frank Sidgwick, founder of Sidgwick & Jackson)

Plot VII Row E Grave 6

MENIN GATE MEMORIAL – SEE NEXT PAGE...

POELCAPELLE BRITISH CEMETERY
8920 Langemark-Poelkapelle, BELGIUM

Poelcapelle British Cemetery is located 10 km nth east of Ieper town centre on the Brugseweg (N313), a road connecting Ieper to Brugge.

Hugh Gordon LANGTON, (1885 – 1917)

2nd Lt, London Regiment, Royal Fusiliers,
Killed 26th October 1917 at Passchendaele.

(Langton was a renowned musician and composer. Unusually, the inscription on his headstone consists of a piece of music).

Special Memorial 3

RAILWAY DUGOUTS BURIAL GROUND (TRANSPORT FARM)
Komenseweg, 8902 Ieper, Belgium

Railway Dugouts Burial Ground (Transport Farm) is located 2 Kms south-east of Ieper town centre, on the Komenseweg, a road connecting Ieper to Komen (N336).

George Upton ROBINS (1878-1915)

Captain, 3 Bn. East Yorkshire Regiment,
Killed in action 5th May 1915

Commemorated Transport Farm Annexe
Memorial A1

MENIN GATE MEMORIAL, Menenstraat, 8900 Ypres, BELGIUM

The Ypres (Menin Gate) Memorial, often referred to simply as the Menin Gate, bears the names of more than 54,000 soldiers who died before 16 August 1917 and have no known grave.

Thomas (Tom) BRANDON (1882-1915)

Private, East Lancs Regiment
Killed at Ypres 13th May 1915

Commemorated on Panel 34

The Hon. Gerald William GRENFELL (1890-1915)

Lieutenant, Rifle Brigade, 2 Bn.
Killed at Ypres, 30th July 1915,

Commemorated on Panel 46-48 & 50

Belgium

Sydney HALE (1891-1915)

Rifleman, 8th Battalion, Rifle Brigade,
Killed 31st July 1915, Zouave Wood,

Commemorated on Panel 46-48 & 50

Note: photo shows Sydney's brother Harold.

John Collinson HOBSON (1893 – 1917),

Lieut, Royal Scots Regiment, tr. Machine Gun Co.
Killed 31st July 1917 at Passchendaele

Commemorated on Panel 56

Walter Scott Stuart LYON (1886-1915)

Lieutenant, Royal Scots Regiment
Killed 8th May 1915 at Ypres

Commemorated on Panel 11

The Hon. Colwyn Erasmus Arnold PHILIPPS
(1888 – 1915) 1st Baron St. Davids and 13th Baronet of Picton

Captain, Royal Horse Guards, Mentioned in
Dispatches. Killed 13th May 1915.

Commemorated on Panel 3

Gerald George SAMUEL (1886 – 1917)

Lieutenant, Queen's Own Royal West Kent Regt
Killed 7th June 1917 at Messines (Mesen)

Commemorated on Panel 45 and 47

TYNE COT MEMORIAL
Vijfwegstraat, 89802, ZONNEBEKE, BELGIUM

The Tyne Cot Memorial to the Missing forms the north-eastern boundary of Tyne Cot Cemetery, which is located 9 kilometres north east of Ieper town centre, on the Tynecotstraat, a road leading from the Zonnebeekseweg (N332).

William Robert HAMILTON (1891 – 1917)

2nd Lt, Coldstream Guards (att Machine Gun Corps), Killed 12th October 1917 at Passchendaele

Commemorated on Panel 9-10

John Ebenezer STEWART, MC, (1888-1918)

Major, 8th Bn Border Regiment, Killed 26th April 1918

Commemorated on Panel 85

Eric Fitzwater WILKINSON, MC (1891 – 1917),

Captain, Leeds Rifles, West Yorkshire Regiment, kia 9th October 1917, Passchendaele

Commemorated on Panel 42 to 47 and 162

(Source: www.tracesofwarwar.com / Photo by Anneke Moerenhout)

VLADSLO GERMAN WAR CEMETERY,
Houtlandstraat 3, 8600 Diksmuide, Belgium

Vladslo German war cemetery is about three kilometres north east of Vladslo, near Diksmuide, Belgium.

After World War II it was decided to merge almost all German war graves from the First World War in West Flanders together in four major cemeteries: Hooglede, Vladslo, Langemarck and Menen.

In all, the German war cemetery Vladslo now contains 25,644 graves from World War I, of which 3.233 were originally buried there. Each stone bears the name of twenty soldiers, with just their name, rank, and date of death.

The cemetery is administered by the German War Graves Commission (*Volksbund Deutsche Kriegsgräberfürsorge*).

The cemetery Vladslo is famous the "Grieving Parents" statues by well known German sculptor Käthe Kollwitz, which she made in the 1930s to commemorate her son Peter who is buried there.

German poet Gerhard Klaus Müller-Rastatt (pen-name Gerhard Moerner) is commemorated in Vladslo Cemetery.

A Seaman - Obermatrose – he was killed on April 15, 1917 in the trenches at Lombartyde, Belgium.

His name can be found on Block 3 Grave 2587

(Thanks to Timo Gälzer for finding Gerhard's resting place.)

VLAMERTINGHE MILITARY CEMETERY, Hospitaalstraat, 8908 Ypres, BELGIUM

Cemetery is located 5 Kms west of Ieper town centre, on the Hospitaalstraat, which is a road leading from the Poperingseweg.

Harold PARRY (1896 – 1917)

2nd Lieut, King's Royal Rifle Corps

Killed 6th May 1917 at Ypres

Plot VI Row L Grave 12

VOORMEZEELE ENCLOSURE NO. 3, Henhuisstraat, 8902 Ypres, BELGIUM

Voormezeele Enclosure No.3 is located 4 Kms south-west of Ieper town centre on the Ruusschaartstraat, a road leading from the Kemmelseweg (connecting Ieper to Kemmel N331).

John BROWN, MC (1891-1819)

Lieut, 6th Seaforth Highlanders Terri .Force.

Killed 11th April 1918 at Wytschaete

Plot XIII Row B Grave 26/27

Also Available By Mail Order!

AGNY MILITARY CEMETERY
rue Marc Lanvin, 62217 Agny, Nord Pas de Calais

Agny is a village in the Department of the Pas-de-Calais immediately south of Achicourt. The Military Cemetery is north-west of the main part of the village across the River Crinchon. The Cemetery is on the outskirts of Agny, on the left hand side of the Achicourt-Wailly road (D3) coming from Arras.

Edward THOMAS (1878 – 1917),
2nd Lieut Royal Garrison Artillery,
Killed in Action Easter Monday, 9th April
1917, Battle of Arras
Row C, Grave 43

ARRAS FLYING SERVICES MEMORIAL
Arras, France

The Arras Flying Services Memorial is in the Faubourg-d'Amiens Cemetery, which is in the Boulevard du General de Gaulle in the western part of the town of Arras.

Arthur Tulloch CULL,
(1887 – 1917)
Captain, Royal Flying
Corps
shot down and killed
11th May 1917

**ARRAS MEMORIAL,
Bd. de General de Gaulle,
62000 Arras, Artois**

Clifford FLOWER, (1891 –
1917), Driver in Royal
Warwickshire Regiment,
kia 20th April 1917, near Lens
Commemorated on Bay 1

Osmund BARTLE WORDSWORTH (1887 – 1917),
2nd Lieut Machine Gun Corps,
Killed 2nd April 1917

Commemorated on Bay 10

Charles Walter BLACKALL, (1876 – 1918),

Lieut Colonel The Buffs, affiliated to The South
Staffordshire Regiment,
Killed 25th March 1918

Commemorated on Bay 2

Bernard PITT, (1881 – 1916),

2nd Lieut Border Regiment,
Killed 30th April 1916

Commemorated on Bay 6

Theodore Percival (T.P.) Cameron WILSON, (1888-
1918)

Captain, Sherwood Foresters,
Killed 23rd March 1918

Commemorated on Bay 10

France

AUBIGNY COMMUNAL CEMETERY
Chemin du Moulin, 62690 AUBIGNY-EN-ARTOIS

Aubigny-en-Artois is a village approximately 15 Kms north-west of Arras on the road (N39) to St. Pol.

Alexander (Alec) Corry Vully de CANDOLE, (1897 – 1918)

Lieut Wiltshire Regiment (att. Machine Gun Corps). Wounded 1917, returned to Western Front. kia 3rd September 1918.

Plot IV Row A Grave 8

Alexander James (Hamish) MANN, (1896-1917)

2nd Lieut 8th (Service) Bn. Black Watch, wounded 9th April 1917, died 10th April 1917.

Plot VI Row A Grave 12

21

AVELUY WOOD (LANCASHIRE DUMP) C'TRY 80300 MESNIL-MARTINSART, France

The Cemetery is about 5 Kms north of the town of Albert and situated in woodland on the eastern side of the road (D50) from Albert to Hamel.

Francis Kennard BLISS, (1892 – 1916), 2nd Lieutenant, Royal Field Artillery, kia 28th September 1916, Thiepval Row J Grave 19

BAILLEUL COMMUNAL CEMETERY EXTENSION NORD, 59270 Bailleul, France

Bailleul is a town in France, near the Belgian border, 14.5 Kms south-west of Ieper and on the main road from St. Omer to Lille.

Frank C. LEWIS, (1898 – 1917), Flight Sub Lieut Royal Naval Air Service, killed 20th August 1917, Ploegsteete Wood

Plot III Row E Grave 223

BAILLEUL ROAD EAST CEMETERY, D919, 62223 Saint-Laurent-Blangy, France

St. Laurent-Blangy is a village adjoining the north-east side of Arras. Leave St. Laurent-Blangy on the D919 towards Bailleul-sire-Berthoult for about 2.5 Kms. Bailleul Road East Cemetery is about 2 Kms north-east of the village on the south side (right) of the road.

Isaac ROSENBERG, (1890 – 1918), Suffolk Regiment, Killed 1st April 1918, near Arras

Special Memorial VC12. (Buried near this spot).

BARLIN COMMUNAL CEMETERY EXT, 101 Chemin Saint-Berlin, 62620 Barlin

Barlin is a village about 11 Kms south-west of Bethune on the D188, between the Bethune-Arras and Bethune-St. Pol roads, about 6.5 Kms south-east of Bruay

William M SCANLAN, MC, MM (1886 – 1917) Canadian, 5th Bn, 1st Canadian Division, Wounded 9th April 1917, died 10th April 1917

Plot I Row H Grave 75

France

BECOURT MILITARY CEMETERY
Rue d'Albert, 80300 Bécordel-Becourt

Becourt is 2 kilometres on the east side of Albert. The Military Cemetery is on the south side of the road from Becourt to Albert.

Hugh Reginald (Rex) FRESTON, (1891 – 1916), 3rd Royal Berkshire Regiment, killed 24th January 1916

Plot I Row E Grave 16

BELLICOURT BRITISH CEMETERY,
Bellicourt, Aisne

Bellicourt is a village 13 Kms north of St. Quentin and 28 Kms south of Cambrai on the N44 road which connects the two cities.

Vivian Telfer PEMBERTON, MC, (1884-1918) Captain, Royal Garrison Artillery, kia 7th October 1918

Plot I Row B Grave 1

BIENVILLERS MILITARY CEMETERY
D2, 62111 Bienvillers-au-Bois

John Hay Maitland HARDYMAN, DSO, MC, (1894-1918) Lieutenant-Colonel, Somerset Light Infantry. Killed 24th August 1918.
(Youngest Lieut-Col in British army at the time of his death)

Plot XIX Row F Grave 11.

BOUZINCOURT COMMUNAL CEMETERY,
Chemin d'Englebelmer, 80300 Bouzincourt

Bouzincourt is a village 3 kilometres north-west of Albert on the road to Doullens (D938).

Donald F GOOLD JOHNSON, (1890–1916),

Lieut 2 Bn Manchester Regiment, Killed 15th July 1916

Plot I Row B Grave 8

BOULOGNE EASTERN CEMETERY, Pas de Calais, France
42 Rue de Dringhen, 62200 Boulogne-sur-Mer, France

Boulogne-sur-Mer is a large Channel port. Boulogne Eastern Cemetery, one of the town cemeteries, lies in the district of St Martin Boulogne, just beyond the eastern (Chateau) corner of the Citadel (Haute-Ville).

The Hon. Julian Henry Francis GRENFELL, DSO, (1888 - 1915)

Captain, 1st Royal Dragoons, wounded 13th May 1915, died 26th May 1915.

Plot II Row A Grave 18

PLEASE ALSO VISIT:

FEARNLEY, Staff Nurse, ETHEL. Queen Alexandra's Imperial Military Nursing Service. Died 23 November 1914. **The first nurse to be killed in WW1**. Mentioned in Dispatches 31st May 1915 (Plot 1 Row B Grave 6)

France

CABARET-ROUGE BRITISH CEMETERY
5000F Rue Carnot, 62153 SOUCHEZ, Pas de Calais

Situated between two war cemeteries, one French and the other German, Cabaret-Rouge British Cemetery lies south of the town of Souchez in France. Cabaret Rouge was a small café, its brick building with red tiles was distinctive in the village where most of the houses were thatched. It stood less than a mile south of Souchez and was destroyed by heavy shelling in May 1915.

Robert Harold BECKH, (1894 – 1916),

2nd Lieut, East Yorkshire Regiment, killed 15th August 1916

Commemorated on: Marquillies Communal Cemetery German Extension Memorial 24

Ivan HEALD, MC, (1883 – 1916),

Lieut. Royal Flying Corps; writer, poet, journalist; killed 4th December 1916.

Plot XV1 Row D Grave 11.

Charles John Beech MASEFIELD, MC, (1882 – 1917),

Prince of Wales North Staffordshire Regiment, kia 2nd July 1917, Lens.
(Cousin of poet John Masefield)

Plot VI Row H Grave 23

France

CATERPILLAR VALLEY CEMETERY D20, 80360 Longueval, Somme

Longueval is a village approximately 13 kilometres east of Albert and 10 kilometres south of Bapaume. The Memorial is situated on a terrace in Caterpillar Valley Cemetery, which lies a short distance west of Longueval, on the south side of the road to Contalmaison.

Hugh STEWART SMITH, (1889 – 1916), Captain, Princess Louise's Argyll and Sutherland Highlanders, killed 18th August 1916

Plot XII Row J Grave 29

CHAUCONIN-NEUFMONTIERS MILITARY CEMETERY, 77 Seine-et-Marne (FRENCH)

Charles PEGUY, French Poet, (1873-1914) Lieutenant in 19th cie French 276th Infantry Regiment kia 5th September 1914 near Villeroy at the Battle of the Marne. There is a memorial to Péguy near the field where he was killed.

CITE BONJEAN MILITARY CEMETERY 54 ave Roger Salengro, 59280 Armentières

Armentières is a town in the Department of the Nord, on the Belgian frontier, 14.5 kilometres north-west of Lille. From the town of Armentières take the D945 to Estaires.

William Ambrose SHORT, CMG (1871-1917) , Lieut Col Royal Field Artillery, kia 21st June 1917 near Armentieres, MID three times and awarded CMG in 1916

Plot VII Row B Grave 20

DEVONSHIRE CEMETERY, MANSEL COPSE, 80300 Mametz, France

Mametz is a village in the Department of the Somme, 6.5 kilometres east of Albert.

William Noel HODGSON, MC (1893 – 1916), Lieut Devonshire Regiment, Killed 1st July 1916, Mametz

Grave A 3

France

DELSAUX FARM CEMETERY, Rue d'Haplincourt, 62124 Beugny, Pas de Calais

This cemetery is near the village of Beugny, 19 kilometres south-west of Cambrai on the Bapaume-Cambrai road (RN30).

David Geoffrey COLLINS (1899-1918)

Guardsman, Grenadier Guards
Died of wounds 11th October 1918

Plot I Row C Grave 29

DUISANS BRITISH CEMETERY, D339, 62181 Etrun, Pas de Calais

Duisans is a village in the Department of the Pas-de-Calais, about 9 kilometres west of Arras.

John Eugene CROMBIE, (1896 – 1917)

Captain 4th Bn. Gordon Highlanders,
Killed 23rd April 1917

Plot IV Row A Grave 22

Funeral of Canadian nurse Gladys Wake who was killed in an air raid on her hospital at Etaples on 21st May 1918 (see page 31)

France

(source www.tracesofwar.com / Anneke Moerenhout)

ESQUELBECQ MILITARY CEMETERY,
Rue du Souvenir, 59470 Esquelbecq, Nord, France

Esquelbecq is a village near the Belgian frontier, 24 kilometres north of Hazebrouck and the same distance south of Dunkirk. The Military Cemetery is about one kilometre west of the village, 200 metres south of the road to Zeggers-Cappel.

Claude Quale Lewis PENROSE, MC and Bar, (1894 – 1918),

Major, Royal Garrison Artillery
Died of wounds 1st August 1918.

Plot III Row D Grave 21

ESTREE-SAINT-DENIS, Oise, Picardie

Jean ARBOUSSET, French Poet (1895-1918)

Sous-lieutenant sapeur au 4e régiment de Génie
Died in combat 9 june 1918 at Cuvilly (Oise).

Buried in the cemetery at Estree Saint Denis

France

ETAPLES MILITARY CEMETERY, D940, 62630 Étaples, Pas de Calais, France

Etaples is a town about 27 kilometres south of Boulogne. The Military Cemetery is to the north of the town, on the west side of the road to Boulogne

Gerrit ENGELKE (1890 – 1918), German Poet; Gefreiter, German Army. Wounded 11 October 1918 at Cambrai.
Taken Prisoner of War. Died 13th October 1918, British Field Hospital, Etaples.
Plot 35 Row B Grave 23

Known as "eat apples" by the Brits, Etaples, Nord Pas de Calais, France, is a port on the River Canche. During WW1 the area was a British Army Base Camp with a training base, a depot for supplies, a detention centre for prisoners, and a centre for the treatment of the sick and wounded, with almost twenty general hospitals.

The camp housed over 100,000 people and the Base Hospitals had facilities for 22,000 patients. All were targets for German bombing raids and in the Cemetery you will find the graves of 19 women who lost their lives, among them Betty Stevenson, the YMCA volunteer killed in the devastating bombing raid on 30th May 1918.

Please go and visit the graves of the women if you visit this cemetery:

BAIN, Nursing Sister, ANNIE WATSON. Mentioned in Despatches. St. John's Ambulance Brigade Hospital, St. John's Ambulance Brigade. Killed in an air raid at Etaples, 1 June 1918. Age 30. Order of St John. Grave Reference: XXVIII. M. 3.

France

CREWDSON, Nursing Sister, DOROTHEA MARY LYNETTE. M M, A R R C. Voluntary Aid Detachment. Died of disease, 12 March 1919. Age 32. Grave Reference: XLV. C. 13.

CROYSDALE, Nursing Sister, MARJORIE. Queen Alexandra's Imperial Military Nursing Service. 2 March 1919. Age 26. Grave Reference: XLV. C. 10.

DAWSON, Matron, EVELINE MAUD. Queen Alexandra's Imperial Military Nursing Service. 10 April 1917. Age 49. Grave Reference: XVII. D. 24.

GREEN, Nursing Sister, MATILDA E.. 7th Canadian Gen. Hosp., Canadian Army Nursing Service. Died of disease, 9 October 1918. Age 32. Grave Reference: XLVIII. A. 10.

HALLAM, Nursing Sister, ALICE VIOLET, 541. Voluntary Aid Detachment. Killed 18 December 1916. Age 45. Grave Reference: I. A. 77.

LOWE, Nursing Sister, Margaret. 1st Canadian Gen. Hosp., Canadian Army Nursing Service. Died of wounds received in German air raid on Etaples, 28 May 1918. Age 32. Grave Reference: XXVIII. M. 9.

LUKER, Worker, DORIS MARY, 6947. Queen Mary's Army Auxiliary Corps. Died of pneumonia, 13 February 1919. Age 21. Grave Reference: LXXII. B. 15.

MACDONALD, Nursing Sister, KATHERINE MAUDE MARY. 1st Canadian Gen. Hosp.Canadian Army Nursing Service. Killed in action, 19 May 1918. Age 31. Grave Reference: XXVIII. L. 8.

MATTHEWS, Worker, MARY MARIA, 47814. Queen Mary's Army Auxiliary Corps. 17 February 1919. Age 28. Grave Reference: LXXII. B. 36.

McARTHUR, Civilian, Miss MARGUERITE MAUDE. Young Men's Christian Association. Died of pneumonia, 13 February 1919. Age 26. while engaged in educational work in France. Grave Reference: XLV. B. 7.

NISBET, Civilian, Eliza Margaret Attd., Scottish Churches Huts. Born 23rd November 1864, Glasgow Died of illness 16 August 1916. Grave Reference: I. B. 43.

PAGE, Worker, BLANCHE AMELIA, 1162. Queen Mary's Army Auxiliary Corps, attd. Signals Sect., Royal Engineers. Died of pneumonia, 7 December 1918. Age 30. Grave Reference: XLVII. B. 16.

ROUTLEDGE, Assistant Forewoman, E H, 1585. Mentioned in Despatches. Queen Mary's Army Auxiliary Corps. Died of pneumonia, 5 March 1919. Age 29. Grave Reference: LXXII. D. 37.

SMITH, Nursing Sister, JEANIE BARCLAY. R R C. Queen Alexandra's Imperial Military Nursing Service. 28 April 1916. Age 42. Died of illness contracted on duty. Grave Reference: I. B. 27

STEVENSON, Civilian, BERTHA GAVIN (BETTY). Young Men's Christian Association. Killed in air raid at Etaples, 30 May 1918. Age 21. Croix de Guerre avec Palme (France). Grave Reference: XXVIII. M. 6.

WAKE, Nursing Sister, GLADYS MAUDE MARY. 1st Canadian Gen. Hosp., Canadian Army Nursing Service. Died of wounds, enemy aircraft action, 21 May 1918. Age 34 Grave Reference: XXVIII. L. 5.

WAKEFIELD, Nursing Sister, JESSIE EMILY. A R R C. Territorial Force Nursing Service. 7 February 1919. Grave Reference: XLV. B. 3.

WHITTAKER, Worker, E, 35663. Queen Mary's Army Auxiliary Corps. 15 February 1919. Grave Reference: LXXII. B. 26.

GROVER, Civilian, FLORENCE VICTORIA. Civilian. Died of pneumonia, 26 November 1918. Age 21. Grave Reference: LI. C. I.

YOU CAN FIND OUT MORE ABOUT THE ROLE OF INSPIRATIONAL WOMEN IN WORLD WAR ONE IN THIS COMPANION BOOK:

NO WOMAN'S LAND

Includes photos and biographies of:

Doctors and Nurses, including Mabel Stobart, Flora Murray, Edith Cavell and Nellie Spindler

Female Fighters, such as Flora Sandes and Milunka Savic

Writers and diarists such as May Sinclair, Mildred Aldridge and Inez Milholland

Plus female spies, female pilots and whole lot more besides!

Compiled by Lucy London / Edited by Paul Breeze
ISBN 978-1-909643-07-9   128 pages
paperback perfect bound

Recommended Retail Price: £10.00
Available via Amazon, poshupnorth.com and all other quality outlets!

France

EUSTON ROAD CEMETERY, 80560 Colincamps, Somme

Colincamps is a village 11 kilometres north of Albert. From Arras take the D919 in the direction of Amiens for 28 kilometres.

Maurice BERTRAND, French poet (1881 - 1914), killed 7th October 1914, Colincamps, Somme, France; from Paris. The French had a military cemetery – Sucrerie Military Cemetery, Colincamps - that was taken over by the British later in WW1 and became Euston Road Cemetery

John William STREETS, (1886 – 1916),

Sergeant York & Lancashire Regiment, Killed 1st July 1916 on the Somme

Special Memorial. A. 6

FLATIRON COPSE CEMETERY, MAMETZ,
Bois Santin, 80300 Bazentin, Somme, Picardie

Flatiron Copse Cemetery is on the right hand side of D929, Amiens-Albert-Bapaume, 10 kilometres east of Albert

Robert STEWART SMYLIE, (1875 – 1916),
Lieutenant Royal Scots Fusiliers, killed 14th July
1916 on the Somme.
(Headmaster County Grammar School, Sudbury, Suffolk, UK)

Special Memorial 3

FRICOURT NEW MILITARY CEMETERY
80300 Fricourt, Somme

The village of Fricourt is approximately 5 kilometres east of Albert. Take the D938 (Albert-Peronne) and turn north 4 kilometres from Albert onto the D147.

Alfred Victor RATCLIFFE, (1887 – 1916)
Lieutenant, West Yorkshire Regiment
Killed on the Somme 1st July 1916

Grave Ref C 8

GROVE TOWN CEMETERY
Mealte, 80300 Bray-sur-Somme

Meaulte is a village just south of Albert. From Albert head south-east on the D329 in the direction of Bray-sur-Somme.

Leslie A. COULSON, (1889 – 1916)
Sergeant, County of London Bn. (The Rangers),
Killed 8th October 1916

Plot 1 Row J Grave 24

France

GUILLEMONT ROAD CEMETERY
D64, 80360 Guillemont, Somme

Guillemont is a village 12 kilometres east of Albert. From the D929 direction Bapaume-Albert take the 2nd turning for Martinpuich, continuing along the D6 for 5 kilometres until the crossroads in the village of Longueval.

The Hon. Raymond ASQUITH (1878 – 1916)

Lieutenant, London Regiment

Killed 15th September 1916 near Ginchy

Plot I Row B Grave 3

Eldest son of British Prime Minister Herbert Asquith (PM 1908-1916)

The Hon Edward Wyndham TENNANT (1897 – 1916)

Lieutenant, Grenadier Guards,

Killed 22nd September 1916

Plot I Row B Grave 18

France

HAC (Honourable Artillery Company) CEMETERY, D956, 62128 Écoust-Saint-Mein, France

H.A.C. Cemetery is about 800 metres south of the village on the west side of the D956 road to Beugenatre.

Arthur Graeme WEST (1891 – 1917)

Captain Oxfordshire and Bucks Light Infantry
Killed 3rd April 1917 near Bapaume

Plot VIII Row C Grave 14

HEILLY STATION CEMETERY
La Couturelle, 80113 Méricourt-l'Abbé, Somme

Mericourt-l'Abbe is a village approx19 km north-east of Amiens and 10 km south-west of Albert. Cemetery is about 2 kilometres south-west of Mericourt-l'Abbe, on the south side of the road to Corbie.

William Eric BERRIDGE, (1894 – 1916)

2nd Lieut 2nd Somerset Light Infantry
Killed 20th August 1916 at Delville Wood

Plot III Row C Grave 18

HERMIES HILL BRITISH CEMETERY,
rue Saint-Michel, 62147 Hermies

Hermies is a town in the Department of the Pas-de-Calais, approx 3.5 km south of the road (D930) from Bapaume to Cambrai

William Oliphant DOWN, MC, (1885 – 1917)

Captain, 4 Bn. Princess Charlotte of Wales's
Royal Berkshire Regiment - killed 22nd May 1917

Special Memorial B 15

HIGHLAND CEMETERY,
62223 ROCLINCOURT, Pas de Calais

Roclincourt is a village a little east of the road from Arras to Lens.

Walter Lightowler WILKINSON, (1885 – 1917),

2nd Lieut ,Princess Louise's 8th Argyll & Sutherland Highlanders Regiment
Killed 9th April 1917, Vimy Ridge

Plot II Row A Grave 5

France

LEBUCQUIERE COMMUNAL CEMETERY EXT
1 Rue du Cimetière, 62124 Lebucquière

Lebucquiere is a village 8 kilometres east of Bapaume and about 2 kilometres south of the main straight road from Bapaume to Cambrai

Robert Ernest (R.E.) VERNEDE (1875 – 1917), 2nd Lieut, 3rd Bn. Rifle Brigade, Killed Eastern Monday, 9th April 1917, Arras

Plot III Row D Grave 16

LIHONS FRENCH NATIONAL CEMETERY
(Nécropole nationale de Lihons) D337, 80320 Lihons

Lihons is a village and commune in the Department of the Somme on the road from Amiens to Nesle. The French National Cemetery is on the north side of this road and on the west side of the Bois Crepey.

Alan SEEGER, (1888 – 1916), American Poet.

Legionnaire (Private) 2nd Foot Regiment, French Foreign Legion - Killed July 1916 on the Somme.

Lies in Ossuary 2 in LIHONS National Cemetery

A statue representing Alan Seeger is on the monument in the Place des États-Unis in Paris, which honours all fallen Americans who volunteered for France during WW1.

LOOS MEMORIAL, 62750 Loose-en-Gohelle, Pas de Calais

The Loos Memorial forms the sides and back of Dud Corner Cemetery.
Loos-en-Gohelle is a village 5 kilometres north-west of Lens

Charles Hamilton SORLEY (1895-1915)

Captain, Suffolk Regiment
Killed near Hulluch, 13th October 1915

Commemorated on Panel 37 & 38

Claude Frank Lethbridge TEMPLER (1895-1918)

Captain, Gloucestershire Regiment
Killed 4th June 1918 near Auchy les Mines

Commemorated on Panel 60 to 64

LOUVENCOURT MILITARY CEMETERY,
2 rue de l'Eglise, 80560 Louvencourt, Somme

Louvencourt is a village 13 km south-east of Doullens on the road (D938)
to Albert. The Cemetery is on the sth-east side of the village.

Rolland Aubrey LEIGHTON (1895-1915)
Lieut, Worcester Regiment,
Died of wounds 23rd Dec 1915, Héburturne.

Plot 1 Row B Grave 20

(Vera Brittain's fiancé; at school with her brother Edward, who was killed on the Italian
Front)

MAZINGARBE COMMUNAL CEMETERY,
31 rue de Carency, 62670 Mazingarbe, Pas de Calais

Mazingarbe is a small town located in the Pas de Calais between the larger town of Lens and Bethune. Mazingarbe Communal Cemetery and Extension is situated adjacent to the Sains-en-Gohelle road from Mazingarbe on the D75

Cyril Morton HORNE, (1885 – 1916),

Captain, King's Own Scottish Borderers,
Killed 27th January 1916 at Mazingarbe

Plot 20

Bernard Freeman TROTTER (1890 – 1917),

Canadian 2nd Lieut in (British) Leicestershire Regt
Killed 7th May 1917

Plot I Row F Grave 13 (Cemetery Extension)

MARTINSART BRITISH CEMETERY,
4 Les Treize, 80300 Mesnil-Martinsart, France

Martinsart is a small village 4 kilometres north of Albert. The cemetery is on the south side of the village on the road (D129) to Aveluy. The cemetery is signposted in the centre of Martinsart.

Frederick Septimus KELLY, DSC (1881-1916)

Lieut Commander Royal Naval Volunteer Res.
KIA 13th November 1916 at Beaucourt-sur-l'Ancre

Plot I Row H Grave 25

Australian-born musician, composer, rower, Olympic Gold Medallist, friend of Rupert Brooke,

France

METZ-EN-COUTURE COMMUNAL CEMETERY
BRITISH EXTENSION, 62124 Metz-en-Couture,

Metz-en-Couture is a village situated in the extreme south-eastern corner of the Department of the Pas-de-Calais. The British Extension is next to the Communal Cemetery and lies adjacent to the D29B

Patrick SHAW-STEWART, (1888 – 1917)
Chevalier of the Legion d'Honneur, Croix de Guerre,

Lieut Comm, Hood Battn, Royal Naval Division,
Killed 30th December 1917, Cambrai

Plot II Row E Grave 1

OISE-AISNE AMERICAN CEMETERY AND
MEMORIAL, D2, 02130 Seringes-et-Nesles

Alfred Joyce KILMER, Cx de Guerre. (1886-1918)

Sergeant with 165 US Infantry Regiment.
Killed 30th July 1918,

Plot B, Row 9, Grave 15.

ORIVAL WOOD CEMETERY
59267 Flesquières

Flesquieres is a village approximately 5 kilometres south-west of Cambrai and about 5 kilometres south of the main road (N30) from Cambrai to Bapaume.

Ewart Alan MACKINTOSH, MC, (1893 – 1917)

Lieutenant, Seaforth Highlanders
Killed 21st November 1917, Cambrai

Plot I Row A Grave 26

ORS VILLAGE COMMUNAL CEMETERY,
Rue de la Gare - 59360 *ORS*

The village of Ors is between Le Cateau and Landrecies. The Communal Cemetery lies to the north-west of the village. It should not be confused with Ors British

Cemetery which is 1 kilometre north-east of the church.

Wilfred Salter OWEN, MC, (1893 – 1918)

Lieutenant Manchester Regiment
Killed 4th November 1918 at Ors

There is also a separate memorial at the nearby Maison Forestiere.

France

OUTTERSTEENE COMMUNAL CEMY EXT,
4548 Route de la Belle Croix, 59270 Bailleul

Outtersteene is a village about 5 km s-west of Bailleul. The Communal Cemetery Extension is n-east of the village on the road to Bailleul.

Louis B. SOLOMON, (1896 – 1918)

Lieutenant, Royal Flying Corps/Royal Air Force, Killed 12th April 1918

Plot IV Row A Grave 57

PERE LACHAISE CEMETERY
20 Avenue Rachel, Montmartre 75018 PARIS

Guillaume APOLLINAIRE, (1880 – 1918),

French Poet, French Army,
Wounded 17th March 1916
Died 9th November 1918

Monument in Division 86

Antoine YVAN, (1880-1914) - French Poet, French Army, Killed 30th August 1914 - Monument in Division 96

POZIERES MEMORIAL,
80300 Ovillers-la-Boisselle

Pozieres is a village 6 km n-east of the town of Albert. The Memorial encloses Pozieres British Cemetery which is a little s-west of the village on the north side of the main road, D929, from Albert to Pozieres.

Colin MITCHELL, (1890 – 1918),

Rifleman, Rifle Brigade
Killed 22nd March 1918 at Fletchin

Commemorated on Panel 81 to 84

SAILLY-SAILLISEL BRITISH CEMETERY
24 Route Nationale 17 80360 Rancourt.

Sailly-Saillisel British Cemetery is 16 kilometres east of Albert and 10 kilometres south of Bapaume. It is on the right hand side (direction Peronne) of the N17 just outside of Sailly Saillisel and before Rancourt.

John Arthur GRAY, DCM (1886 – 1917)

2nd Lieut, Royal Berkshire Regiment
Kia 4th March 1917, near Bapaume.

Plot VII. Row A. Grave 7.

ST. PATRICK'S CEMETERY, LOOS
22 Rue Alexandre Maniez 62750 Loos-en-Gohelle

Loos (Loos-en-Gohelle) is a village to the north of the N43 road from Lens to Bethune. Arriving at Loos, turn right at CWGC sign post.

Arthur Keedwell HARVEY-JAMES (1875-1917)

Captain (Buffs) Royal East Kent Regiment
Killed in action 15th April 1917

Plot III Row A Grave 6

Better known as actor, writer and silent film star Arthur Scott Craven.

France

ST. SEVER CEMETERY, ROUEN,
Boulevard Stanislas Girardin, 76140 Le Petit-Quevilly, Rouen

St Sever Cemetery and St Sever Cemetery Extension are located within a large communal cemetery situated on the eastern edge of the southern Rouen suburbs of Le Grand Quevilly and Le Petit Quevilly.

Richard Molesworth DENNYS (1884 – 1916)

Captain, Loyal North Lancashire Regiment
Wounded 12th July at Tara Redoubt on the Somme, died 24th July 1916 in Rouen Hospital

Grave Reference: Officers A 4 7

Francis St. Vincent MORRIS (1896 – 1917)

2nd Lieut, No. 3 Squadron, Royal Flying Corps (att Sherwood Foresters)
Crash landed at Vimy Ridge and died on the operating table at military hospital in Rouen 29th April 1917

Grave Ref: Officers B 6 5

PLEASE ALSO VISIT THE WOMEN CASUALTIES WHO ARE BURIED IN ST SEVER CEMETERY!

KNOX, Sister, HILDA MARY. - Australian Army Nursing Service.
Died of sickness, 17 February 1917. Age 33. Grave Reference: Officers, B. 4. 10

DICKSON, Nurse, MARY Charlotte.. Voluntary Aid Detachment. Died of meningitis, 16 February 1917. Age 30. Grave Reference: Officers, B. 4. 9.

PEARTON, Worker, EDITH. Young Men's Christian Association.
Died 13 March 1918. Grave Reference: Officers, B. 4. 17.

RIGGALL, LOUISA Blanche. Australian Red Cross Society. MID. Died of cerebral haemorrage, 31 August 1918, age 50. Grave Reference: Officers, B. 3. 1.
Riggall was an academic painter who enjoyed early success in her career both in Melbourne and Paris

SMITH LEE, Nurse, JEANNIE. 30th (Northumberland) Detachment attd. 9th Gen. Hosp., Voluntary Aid Detachment. Died of sickness, 30 March 1917. Age 25.
Grave Reference: Officers, B. 5. 25

WARNOCK, Nurse, ELIZABETH McMATH (DAISY). 10th (Glasgow) Detachment attd. 8th General Hospital, Voluntary Aid Detachment. Born 1887 Died of septicaemia, 5 May 1918. Age 31. Grave Reference: Officers, B. 4. 23.

BRANFOOT, Civilian, Dame LUCY INNES. Civilian, Lady Mabelle Egerton's Coffee Stall, St. Sever Station. Died of bronchitis, 16 March 1916. Age 52. Grave Reference: Officers, A. 2. 6.

ST. SEVER CEMETERY EXTENSION, ROUEN,

ARMSTRONG, Sister, ELLEN. R R C, Mentioned in Despatches. Reserve, Queen Alexandra's Imperial Military Nursing Service. 20 March 1919. Age 38.
Grave Reference: S. V. M. 6.

BOUSFIELD, Nurse, MARY CAWSTON. Mentioned in Despatches, A R R C. 8th Gen. Hosp., Voluntary Aid Detachment. Died of pneumonia contracted on duty, 24 February 1919. Age 27. Grave Reference: S. V. M. 10.

GOSLING, Worker, CLARA, 2108. Queen Mary's Army Auxiliary Corps. 7 November 1918. Grave Reference: S. V. J. 12.

HOLBOROW, Forewoman, ROSE MABEL, 1923. Queen Mary's Army Auxiliary Corps, attd. 1st Base Mechanical Transport Depot.. 5 October 1918. Age 36
Grave Reference: S. V. H. 3.

JOHNSTON, Telephonist, ELIZABETH Sligh., 18375. Queen Mary's Army Auxiliary Corps. 25 December 1918. Age 27. Grave Reference: S. V. L. 10.

LLEWELLYN, Nurse, GWYNEDD VIOLET. 126 (Somerset) Detachment attd. No. 2 Hospital, Voluntary Aid Detachment. Died of influenza, 3 November 1918. Age 19.
Grave Reference: S. V. G. 13.

STEELE, Worker, WINIFRED MARY, 1593. Queen Mary's Army Auxiliary Corps. Died of pnuemonia, 9 December 1918. Age 27. Grave Reference: S. V. L. 7.

SERRE ROAD CEMETERY NO. 2, BEAUMONT-HAMEL, D919, 62116 Hébuterne,

The village of Serre is 11 kilometres north-north-east of Albert. Using the D919 from Arras to Amiens you will drive through the villages of Bucquoy, Puisieux then Serre-les-Puisieux (approximately 20 kilometres south of Arras).

Henry Lionel FIELD, (1894 – 1916),
2nd Lieut, Royal Warwickshire Regiment
Killed 1st July 1916 on the Somme
Plot II Row C Grave 10

Gilbert WATERHOUSE, (1883 – 1916),
2nd Lieut, Essex Regiment
Killed 1st July 1916 on the Somme
Plot I Row K Grave 23

France

TERLINCTHUN BRITISH CEMETERY, WIMILLE,
Pas de Calais, France

Terlincthun British Cemetery is situated on the northern outskirts of Boulogne. From Calais follow the A16 to Boulogne, come off at Junction 32 and follow the D96E for Wimereux Sud. Continue on this road for approximately 1 kilometre when the Cemetery will be found on the left hand side of the road.

Cecil Edward CHESTERTON (1879 – 1918), Private, Highland Light Infantry; wounded Western Front several times. Died on 6th December 1918. Plot XII. Row B. Grave 38.

(Writer, journalist, poet. - younger brother of G.K. Chesterton)

And don't forget to visit these women who are also buried in Terlincthun:

BARROW, Worker, MARGARET ANN, 36156. Queen Mary's Army Auxiliary Corps. Died of disease, 3 November 1918. Age 24. Grave Reference: IX. C. 21.

HALL, Worker, ANNIE, 11900. Queen Mary's Army Auxiliary Corps. 23 March 1919. Age 30. Grave Reference: XV. B. 35.

INGRAM, Nurse, EDITH. 55th Gen. Hosp., Voluntary Aid Detachment. Died 14 August 1918. Age 31. Grave Reference: II. C. 27.

France

KING, Nursing Sister, Jessie Nelson. 3rd Canadian Gen. Hosp., Canadian Army Medical Corps. She died on April 4th, **1919** at the 14th Stationary Hospital in Boulogne at the age of 26 (cerebro spinal meningitis). Grave Reference: XIV. A. 2.

MASSEY, Worker, Florence E M T, 1229. Queen Mary's Army Auxiliary Corps. 1 December 1918. Grave Reference: XII. A. 32.

McKAY, Nursing Sister, Evelyn Verrall . 3rd Canadian Gen. Hosp., Canadian Army Medical Corps. She died on November 4th from a broncho-pneumonia at the age of 26. Grave Reference: VII. C. 26.

PARNELL, Worker, Elsie, 36840. Queen Mary's Army Auxiliary Corps. Died of disease, 6 March 1919. Age 23. Grave Reference: XV. B. 2.

SPITTLE, Worker, MARY ANNIE , 1667. Queen Mary's Army Auxiliary Corps. 12 February 1919. Age 26. Grave Reference: XIII. C. 41.

YOUNG, Nurse, MARGARET CAMERON. 2nd Gen. Hosp., Voluntary Aid Detachment. Died of disease, 30 July 1918. Age 25. Grave Reference: I. F. 44.

Find out more about the heroic female nurses, doctors, drivers and other workers who were killed and buried on the Western Front:

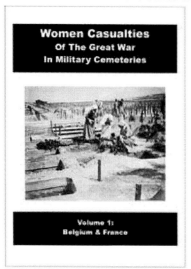

Women Casualties Of The Great War In Military Cemeteries

Volume 1: Belgium & France

The information contained in this book has been compiled from the websites of – among others - the Commonwealth War Graves Commission, American Battle Monuments Commission & various Scottish, Australian and Canadian resources and archives. It is all available to view completely free of charge on their various websites if you have the time to wade through them all to find specific details.

We have, however, brought together details of the graves of women who were killed on the Western Front during WW1 into one handy volume along with brief details about the cemeteries and some of the organisations that the women served with.

ISBN 978-1-909643-26-0

86 pages paperback

Recommended Retail Price: £7.50

Available by mail order via Amazon, from www. poshupnorth.com - and all good bookshops!

THIEPVAL MEMORIAL 8 Rue de l'Ancre, 80300 Thiepval,

George Sainton Kaye Butterworth MC (1885-1916)

2nd Lieutenant, Durham Light Infantry,
Killed 5th August 1916. British composer.

Commemorated on Pier and Face 14A and 15C

Percy HASELDEN, (1895 – 1916),

Private, King's Liverpool Regiment
Killed 30th July 1916

Commemorated on Pier and Face 1D 8B and 8C.

Thomas Michael KETTLE (1880 – 1916)

Lieutenant, Royal Dublin Fusiliers
Killed 9th September 1916 at Ginchy

Commemorated on Pier and Face 16 C

Hector Hugh MUNRO ('Saki') (1870 – 1916)
Lance Sgt, Royal Fusiliers
Killed 13th November 1916 at Beaumont - Hamel
Commemorated on Pier and Face 8 C 9 A and 16 A

Alexander ROBERTSON, (1882 – 1916),
Corporal, Sheffield Bn., York & Lancaster Reg.
Killed 1st July 1916
Commemorated on Pier and Face 14A & 14B

Nicholas Herbert TODD, (1878 – 1916),
Rifleman London Regiment
Killed 7th October 1916
Commemorated on Pier and Face 9C

Bernard Charles De Boismaison WHITE, (1886 – 1916),
Lieut, Tyneside Scottish Bn. Northumberland Fusiliers,
Killed 1st July 1916
Commemorated Pier and Face 10 B 11 B and 12 B.

Cyril W. WINTERBOTHAM, (1887 – 1916),
Lieut, Gloucestershire Regiment,
Killed 27th August 1916
Commemorated on Pier and Face 5 A and 5 B

VAUX EN AMIENOIS COMMUNAL CEMETERY

Vaux-en-Amienois is a small village in the Department of the Somme, 8 kilometres north-west of Amiens along the D933 and left on the D97

John Watt SIMPSON, (1888-1916)

2nd Lieut, Border Regiment

Killed 8th December 1916, Amiens

Grave Ref: A 4

VERMANDOVILLERS GERMAN WAR CEMETERY, D143 80320, Somme

Alfred LICHTENSTEIN, (1889 – 1914),

German Writer and Poet,

Bavarian 2nd Infantry Kronprinz Regiment

killed 25th September 1914

near Vermandovillers

Reinhard SORGE, (1892 – 1916),

German writer and poet,

6th Company of 69th Reserve Infantry Regiment - part of the 15th Reserve Division

Killed 20th July 1916 at Ablaincourt

VILLERS STATION CEMETERY, Pas de Calais 62144 Villers-au-Bois, France

Villers-au-Bois is a village in the Department of the Pas-de-Calais, 11 km north-west of Arras. The Cemetery is about 2 km north-west of the village along a track from the Villers-au-Bois to Servins road (D65).

James MILES LANGSTAFF (1883 – 1917),

Major, 76 Bn. Canadian Infantry,

Killed 1st March 1917 near Vimy Ridge

Plot Vii Row D Grave 2

France

VIS-EN-ARTOIS MEMORIAL / MILITARY CEMETERY
1 Route Nationale, 62156 Haucourt, France

Vis-en-Artois and Haucourt are villages on the straight main road from Arras to Cambrai about 10 kilometres south-east of Arras. The Memorial is the back drop to the Vis-en-Artois British Cemetery, which is west of Haucourt on the north side of the main road.

John Stephen Marcus BAKER (1897-1918)

Private / Signaller, 7th London Regiment

Killed 8th August 1918 at Morlancourt

Commemorated on Panel 10 of the Memorial

Henry Lamont SIMPSON (1897-1918)

2nd Lieut, Lancashire Fusiliers

Killed 29th August 1918 at Hazebrouck

Commemorated on Panel 5 and 6 of the Memorial

WANCOURT BRITISH CEMETERY,
1 Rue d'Alsace, 62128 Wancourt, France

Wancourt is a village about 8 kilometres south-east of Arras. It is 2 kilometres south of the main road from Arras to Cambrai

William Henry LITTLEJOHN, (1891 – 1917)

Company Sergeant Major, Middlesex Regiment

Killed 10th April 1917

Plot V Row E Grave 16

WARLINCOURT HALTE BRITISH CEMETERY,
62158 Saulty, Pas de Calais

Warlincourt and Saulty are villages on either side of the main road (N25) between Arras (22 kilometres) and Doullens (13 kilometres).

Geoffrey Bache SMITH, (1894 – 1916)

Lieutenant, Lancashire Fusiliers

Killed 3rd December 1916

Plot III Row G Grave 2

France

WIMEREUX COMMUNAL CEMETERY, 37B Rue René Cassin, 62930 Wimereux, Pas de Calais

Wimereux is a small town situated approximately 5 kilometres north of Boulogne.

From the centre of Boulogne take the A16 to Calais and exit at junction 33. Follow the D242 into Wimereux and at the first roundabout in town, take the third exit, continuing on the D242 and after approximately 200 yards, turn left into a one way road. The Cemetery lies at the end of this road.

John McCRAE (1872-1918)

Lieut Colonel, Canadian Medical Corps and Canadian Royal Artillery
Killed 28th January 1918

Plot IV Row H Grave 3

(McCrae's famous poem "In Flanders Fields" inspired American WW1 poet Moina Belle Michael's always wear a red poppy in remembrance campaign)

France

PLEASE VISIT THE WOMEN WHO ARE ALSO BURIED AT WIMEREUX:

CLAYTON-SWAN, Civilian, MILDRED. Army Service Corps (Canteens). 24 February 1917. Grave Reference: III. G. 2.

COLE, Sister, EMILY HELENA. Queen Alexandra's Imperial Military Nursing Service. 21 February 1915. Age 32. Daughter of Mrs. E. H. Cole, of 46, Charminster Rd., Bournemouth. Grave Reference: III. Q. 1.

DUNCAN, Sister, ISABELLA LUCY MAY. 13th Stat. Hosp., Queen Alexandra's Imperial Military Nursing Service. 1 March 1917. Grave Reference: III. F. 2.

EVANS, Member, MARGARET ELLEN. 83rd Gen. Hosp, Voluntary Aid Detachment. 22 July 1917. Age 39. Grave Reference: III. A. 1.

HOCKEY, Sister, JESSIE OLIVE. Reserve, Queen Alexandra's Imperial Military Nursing Service. South African 14 August 1917. Age 32. Reference: III. A. 3.

KING, Member, NITA MADELINE. Voluntary Aid Detachment. 25 May 1917. Age 29. Grave Reference: III. B. 4.

LANCASTER, Nurse, ALICE HILDA. Special Military Probationer attd., Territorial Force Nursing Service. Drowned whilst bathing, 3 June 1918. Age 35. Grave Reference: IV. A. 2.

PICKARD, Volunteer, Mrs. RUBIE. Voluntary Aid Detachment. 13 April 1916. Age 67. Wife of Capt. Pickard, of St. Leonard, Pont de Briques, Pas de Calais, France. B.R.C. voluntary worker in Newspaper Dept. for supplying British hospitals with daily papers. Grave Reference: III. L. 3.

St. JOHN, Member, BARBARA ESMEE, Sussex/112. Voluntary Aid Detachment. Died of Landry's paralysis, 12 October 1916. Age 31. Grave Reference: III. I. 4.

TREVELYAN, Civilian, ARMOREL KITTY. Army Service Corps (Canteens). Died of measles and pneumonia, 27 February 1917. Age 19. Daughter of Mrs. Trevelyan (now Sinclair) and the late Capt. Walter Raleigh Trevelyan, of Furry Park, Raheny, Co. Dublin. Grave Reference: III. F. 4.

WHITELY, Nursing Sister, ANNA E.. 10th Canadian Stat. Hosp., Canadian Army Nursing Service. Born 22.1.1872 – Died 21 April 1918. Grave Reference: IV. A. 1.

WILSON, Sister, CHRISTINA MURDOCH. Queen Alexandra's Imperial Military Nursing Service. Died of pneumonia, Born 21.8.1873 - 1 March 1916. Age 42. Daughter of the late Thomas and Agnes Park Wilson, of Glasgow. Grave Reference: III. L. 4.

WILSON, Sister, MYRTLE ELIZABETH. Queen Alexandra's Imperial Military Nursing Service. Died of pneumonia, 23 December 1915. Age 38. Grave Reference: III. M. 1.

Also Available By Mail Order!

POETS, WRITERS & ARTISTS ON THE SOMME 1916

Includes brief biographies and examples of work by poets and writers who were

Killed on the First Day of the Battle of the Somme

And those killed on wounded or present during the 1916 Somme Offensive

A Centenary Collection Compiled by Lucy London

ISBN: 9781909643246 - 140 Pages Paperback - RRP £10.00

Available via Amazon, poshupnorth.com and all other quality outlets!

POETS' GRAVES AND MEMORIALS ELSEWHERE IN THE WORLD

BASRA WAR MEMORIAL, IRAQ

Note: The Commonwealth War Graves Commission (and us as well...!) strongly advise that the Foreign and Commonwealth Office should be contacted before attempting to visit Iraq.

Ivar CAMPBELL (1890-1916)

Captain, 3rd Battalion, Argyll and Sutherland Highlanders attached 1st Battalion, Seaforth Highlanders; Died of wounds received in action at Sheikh Saad 8th January 1916.

Commemorated on Panel 41 of Basra Memorial

Gerald Caldwell SIORDET MC (1885 – 1917)

Second Lieut, Rifle Brigade
Killed 9th February 1917, Kut-al-Amara

Commemorated on Panel 41 of Basra Memorial

Please also remember:

Sister, Florence, NARRELLE Jessie HOBBES (Australian). Queen Alexandra's Imperial Military Nursing Service. Taken ill and buried at sea, 10 May 1918. Age 37.
Commemorated on Panel 43 of Basra Memorial

Although at the time of writing it is inadvisable to travel to Iraq to try to find the following, we nevertheless wanted to include them and honour their memory. These women are buried in military cemeteries in Iraq, although we believe that these sites are currently unaccessible.

AMARA WAR CEMETERY, Iraq:
TREVETHAN, Staff Nurse, R. Territorial Force Nursing Service. 4 September 1917. Grave Reference: XIV. A. 30.

BAGHDAD (NORTH GATE) WAR CEMETERY, Iraq
JONES, Chief Matron, BEATRICE ISABEL. C B E, R R C. Queen Alexandra's Imperial Military Nursing Service. 14 January 1921. Age 54. Nightingale International Medal. Grave Reference: VIII. L. 11.

BASRA WAR CEMETERY, Iraq:
- BLACKLOCK, Nursing Sister, ALICE MAY. Territorial Force Nursing Service. 13 August 1916. Age 30. Grave Reference: V. N. 12.
- COMPTON, Sister, FLORENCE D'OYLY. 65th British Gen. Hosp., Queen Alexandra's Imperial Military Nursing Service. Drowned, 15 January 1918. Age 29. Grave Reference: I. G. 12.
- FAITHFULL, Nurse, FLORENCE MARY. 65th British Gen Hosp., Voluntary Aid Detachment. Drowned, 15 January 1918. Age 26. Grave Reference: I. G. 14.
- KEARNEY, Nursing Sister, I M. Queen Alexandra's Imperial Military Nursing Service. 26 September 1916. Grave Reference: V. R. 14.
- KEMP, Staff Nurse, C M F. 40th British Gen. Hosp., Queen Alexandra's Imperial Military Nursing Service. 4 July 1918. Grave Reference: III. T. 2.
- ROBINSON, Sister, ELIZABETH. 3rd Brit. Gen. Hosp., Territorial Force Nursing Service. Died of malaria, 12 July 1919. Grave Reference: II. D. 2.
- TINDALL, Sister, Fanny. Reserve, Queen Alexandra's Imperial Military Nursing Service, Killed 15 January 1918. Grave Reference: I. G. 11.
- Sister Alice Welford, Reserve, Queen Alexandra's Imperial Military Nursing Service attd. 65th Brit. Gen. Hospital. Killed 15 January 1918. Grave Reference: I G 13

KOPRIVSHTITSA, BULGARIA
Dimcho Debelyanov St 6, Koprivshtitsa 2077,

Dimcho DEBELYANOV (1887-1916) Bulgarian Army. Killed 2nd October 1916 near Gorno Karadjvo. His body was taken to Koprivshtitsa for re-burial in 1931.

The family home is now a museum and there is a memorial tombstone with the sculpture "Grieving Mother" at Dimcho Debelyanov's grave by the sculptor Ivan Lazarov (1890 – 1952).

PROSECCO FIRST WORLD WAR AUSTRO-HUNGARIAN CEMETERY, ITALY
Strada Provinciale 1, 34121 Prosecco, Trieste

Robert ZELLERMEYER, (1888 – 1917), Austro-Hungarian Poet and airman; killed 5th February 1917.

Grave Reference: B3/53

EISENACH, Germany
Hauptfriedhof, Friedhofstraße, 99817 Eisenach.

Walter FLEX, (1887 – 1917), German. Leutnant in 3. Niederschlesischen Infanterie-Regiment Nr. 50. Killed 16th October 1917 at Peudehof, Saaremaa Island (formerly Ösel Island), Estonia

Original burial place destroyed – symbolic memorial erected in graveyard in his home town of Eisenach.

GREEN HILL CEMETERY, SULVA BAY, GALLIPOLI, TURKEY

Nowell OXLAND (1891-1915) Lieut 6th Border Regiment, Killed on 9th August 1915 at Suvla Bay.

Plot I Row C Grave 7

**Rupert Chawner Brooke
(1887 - 1915)**

Sub-Lieutenant, Royal Naval
Volunteer Reserve.

Served during the evacuation from
Antwerp in 1914. Hood Battalion.
Died of sickness on the voyage to
Gallipoli on 23rd April 1915.

Buried in an isolated grave on
Skyros Island, Greece

RUPERT BROOKE & SKYROS
by Lucy London

Rupert Brooke was already a well known and published poet before
the First World War. He was commissioned into the Royal Naval
Volunteer Reserve as a Sub-Lieutenant, joining the Hood Battalion,
2nd Brigade, R.N. Division and took part in the Royal Naval
Division's expedition to Antwerp in Belgium.

Rupert's Division set sail from Avonmouth near Bristol for Gallipoli in
the Union-Castle Line ship "Grantully Castle" which had been
converted for use as a troopship. Among the ships escorting the
flotilla of over 200 ships heading for Gallipoli was the Dreadnought
Battleship "The Prince George".

The ships put into Cairo in Egypt, where Rupert became seriously ill
with a fever and dysentery. An initial landing at Gallipoli was
postponed and the ships were diverted to islands in the Aegean Sea.

Transmission by post permitted by the Postmaster General.

H.M. Hospital Ship "GRANTULLY CASTLE" *(Publication Officially sanctioned by the Lords Commissioners of the Admiralty)*

.When the "Grantully Castle" arrived in the Aegean, the anchorage at Lemnos was already already full of ships, so Rupert's ship put into Trebouki Bay off the Island of Skyros.

Skyros is to the east of the mainland of Greece and is one of the Sporades Archipelago in the Aegean Sea (sporades being Greek for "those scattered"). Rupert and the other members of the Hood Battalion went ashore on Skyros for manoeuvres. They were resting in a small olive grove about 300 metres above sea level, when Rupert was stung on the face" by "a little grey fly" and his health, already impaired, deteriorated rapidly.

According to her log, the French Naval Hospital Ship " 'Duguay-Trouin' was at anchor in the bay at Trebouki Bay, having taken on coal in Alexandria", when Rupert Brooke was transferred to her by cutter from the "Grantully Castle".

Rupert was described as "...a Lieutenant on General Hamilton's staff". The Log continues "Wireless messages come in. General Hamilton and Winston Churchill are worrying."

In spite of the efforts of "the whole medical staff mobilised for the single patient" (as there were no wounded for them to treat at that stage, Rupert died on 23rd April England has lost her greatest poet".

Arrangements had to be made speedily for Rupert's burial as orders had come through to proceed to the Dardanelles. Rupert had commented upon the tranquility and beauty of the Olive Grove in which the troops had rested during manoeuvres so it seemed the ideal place to bury him.

The log of the "Duguay-Trouin" described the funeral as follows: "The coffin is placed on the poop and covered with the English flag. Sixteen palms decorate improvised chapel. The officers of the "Duguay-Trouin" lay on the coffin a bunch of wild flowers stolen from the bees of the Island and with the French colours" (red, white and blue) "At the foot of the coffin stands a sailor presenting arms. Lieutenant Arthur Asquith (1883 - 1939 - one of the sons of Herbert Henry Asquith, the British Prime Minister in the early days of the War) , who has not left his friend for a moment, is at the side of the bier with some other English officers. A brief twilight. Then night falls."

As there was "no time to engrave a brass plate, the Lieutenant calls for a soldering iron. Then, by the light of the lamps which are like a wreath of watch lights, he scars on the oak plank itself these letters

RUPERT BROOKE

A sharp whistle is heard. The ship's company lines up with bared heads to pay the last honours. A launch takes the boat which carried the coffin in tow. Other boats pull off from the (other British) warships ("Campus" "Prince George" and "Prince Edward"). There are many of them."

"Some olive trees in a more fertile hollow. At their foot a grave has been dug."

Rupert Brooke's original grave on Skyros

William Denis Browne, the composer, critic and pianist (who was known as Denis) was one of Rupert's friends and was also at Rupert's side when he died. Denis, commissioned into the Royal Naval Division at the same time as Rupert, was killed in Gallipoli on 4th June 1915.

Another friend present was Forgotten Poet Patrick Shaw-Stewart, who played an important role in Rupert's funeral being in charge of the firing party and was himself killed on the Western Front in December 1917.

Other members of the Hood Battalion group "Latin Club", as the Rupert Brooke circle was called, who were present at Rupert's funeral, were

- Charles Lister (son of Lord Ribblesdale), who died after being wounded at Gallipoli in August 1915,

- Bernard Freyberg, VC (1889 - 1963) who transferred to the British Army - Queen's (Royal West Surrey) Regiment - in May 1916, and

- Frederick Septimus Kelly*, Australian/British musician/composer, who was wounded twice at Gallipoli and killed on the Western Front in November 1916.

After the First World War, Stanley Casson was working as Deputy Director at the British School of Archaeology in Athens when he was approached by a friend at the British Legation regarding the placing of a tomb over the grave of Rupert Brooke.

Rupert's mother had commissioned a specially sculpted marble grave in memory of her son. Casson was the ideal person, with his knowledge of Greek sculpture, to organise and supervise the transport and construction of the two and a half tons of marble and iron railings that you will see if you visit Brooke's grave today.

The logistics of the operation were quite remarkable and are detailed in a book called "Steady Drummer" written by Stanley Casson and published in 1935 by G. Bell of London. Lady MacLellan has kindly sent me a copy of the section concerning the grave of Rupert Brooke. Casson had to hire a boat to transport the marble, then get to the island himself. Once there, he had to build a small jetty for the unloading of the seven or so crates containing the marble. Once on land, there was the problem of getting the crates up the hill to the site of the grave via the only road which, at that time was a rough goat track.

Nothing daunted, Casson cut wooden rollers from pine trees and began to level the track by removing outcrops of rock on the path. That alone took over a week. Then the crates had to be pushed up the track and Casson mentioned how much he admired and respected the architects of Stonehenge. During the evenings, Casson spent time with his hosts the local shepherds and goatherds on the island who offered him hospitality and shelter in their shack. After a supper of bread and milk, they would sit round an open fire, talking about the war with the shepherds, some of whom had served in a Greek Division sent to Odessa with other Allied troops.

Returning briefly to Athens to fetch some tools to complete the task, Casson enlisted the help of the author Norman Douglas who had just arrived there. The pair returned to Skyros and oversaw the completion of the laying of marble tomb over Brooke's grave. Finally, Casson had the tomb consecrated by the head of the local monastery of St. George.

Brooke's replacement grave on Skyros (Photo by Commonwelath War Graves Commission)

Casson reflected sadly: "I wondered what Brooke would have thought to see this strange assembly. I came away sadly to think that here was still another of my generation accounted for. It was a lonely world now for men of my age."

Casson arranged to have the original wooden crosses that had marked Rupert's grave on Skyros sent back to the Brooke family in Rugby, where they were put on the family burial plot. By 2008 the crosses had weathered and were replaced. The originals are now at Rugby School.

Rupert Brooke's WW1 poetry collections were:
"Collected Poems" published by Lane, New York, 1915; "Collected Poems with a memoir by Edward Marsh", published by Sidgwick & Jackson, 1918 and "Collected Poems" published by the Medici Society in 1919.

*While at Gallipoli, Frederick Septimus Kelly, who was awarded the DSC, wrote his "Elegy for a String Orchestra "In Memoriam Rupert Brooke"

Stanley Casson *(1889 – 1944)*
British Solder Poet In Two World Wars

In 1914 Casson joined the East Lancs Regiment and was posted to France. He was shot in the leg at Ypres in 1915. After recovering, he served in the Balkans and was awarded the Greek Order of the Savior for services to Greece.

To help his recovery after the war, he left Oxford and became Assistant Director of the British School in Athens. During his time there, he constructed the marble grave on the island of Skyros for Rupert Brooke.

When The Second World War started in 1939, Casson was already in the Army Reserve and joined the Intelligence Service as a Major. He narrowly avoided capture by the Germans when they invaded Holland in 1940. Soon after, he served with the British Military Mission to Greece, escaping again to Crete and thence to Cairo.

Back in London, with the rank of Lieutenant Colonel, Casson worked in the SOE for the Greek Resistance.

In April 1944, six weeks before D-Day, SOE deployed him to Greece for the Liberation with a mission to mediate with Monarchists and Communists in an attempt to prevent the eventual civil war. On take-off from Cornwall, the RAF Transport Command aircraft, crashed into the sea, killing all on board.

This information has been kindly supplied by Lt. Colonel Casson's daughter, Jennifer MacLellan, who has given permission for us to reproduce it.

Stanley Casson (1889-1944) - Lieutenant Colonel, Intelligence Corps is buried in Newquay (Fairpark) C of E Cemetery: E Plot, Cons Grave 684.

Above: Chatham Naval Memorial

POETS' GRAVES AND MEMORIALS IN THE UNITED KINGDOM

ABERDEEN SPRING BANK CEMETERY
Countesswells Rd, Aberdeen AB15 7YH

Henry Brian BROOKE, (1889 – 1916),

Captain Gordon Highlanders
wounded and sent to Britain for treatment. Died 25th July 1916

Grave Ref: N18

CHATHAM NAVAL MEMORIAL
61 King's Bastion, Gillingham Kent ME7 5DQ

Miles Jeffery GAME DAY, DFC, (1896 – 1918),
Flight Commander, Royal Naval Air Service
Killed 27th February 1918 over Dunkirk

Commemorated on Panel 30.

Also on WAR MEMORIAL ST. JOHN'S COLLEGE, CAMBRIDGE

RICHMOND CEMETERY
Grove Road, Richmond Surrey TW10 5BJ

Arthur Lewis JENKINS, (1892 – 1917)
Lieutenant, Royal Flying Corps,
killed 31st December 1917
Grave ref: M1497

RAKE LANE CEMETERY, WALLASEY
Rake Lane, Wallasey, CH45 5LD

Arthur Geoffrey Nelson WALL 1897 – 1917)
2nd Lieut, Royal Flying Corps,
Killed 6th August 1917
Grave: NC 10 101

SHOTWICK (ST. MICHAEL'S) CHURCHYARD
Shotwick Lane, Shotwick, Cheshire CH1 6HX

Horace Edgar Kingsmill Bray (1896- 1918)
Canadian
2nd Lt. 67 Training Squadron, Royal Air Force
Killed in accident 9th July 1918 at Shotwick

Grave located in north west part of cemetery

ALSO AVAILABLE FROM THE SAME PUBLISHER

Female Poets Of The First World War - Volume 2
Lucy London

FEMALE POETS – VOLUME 1
ISBN 978-1-909643-02-4 RRP £10.00
126 pages paperback with b/w photographs

FEMALE POETS - VOLUME 2
ISBN 978-1-909643-17-8 RRP £10.00
186 pages paperback with b/w photographs

SELECTED POEMS 2012
Edited by Paul Breeze
ISBN 978-0-9539782-7-4
74 pages paperback

Purple Patches
ISBN: 978-1-909643-00-0
42 pages paperback

Guns & Pencils
ISBN: 978-0-9539782-2-9
26 pages paperback

Blackpool To Bond Street!
ISBN: 978-0-9539782-5-0
60 pages paperback

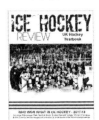

**Fylde Flyers –
A Complete Record**
ISBN 978-1-909643-13-0
150 pages paperback

**The Seagull Has Landed
(Blackpool Seagulls)**
ISBN 978-1-909643-01-7
84 pages paperback

A Year In the Wild
ISBN 978-1-909643-19-2
160 pages paperback

**Ice Hockey Review
UK Hockey Yearbook &
NIHL Yearbook**
For years available – see
www.icehockeyview.co.uk

*Available to order from numerous outlets, including: www.poshupnorth.com,
.amazon, www.icehockeyreview.co.uk
The Wilfred Owen Story, Birkenhead and all good bookshops.*

The World's Best FREE TO ENTER
Poetry and Art Competition

Judging Categories:

Under 18
UK & Ireland Adult
Overseas Adult
Photographic
Competition

In Photo: 2012 Under 18 Winner
Meredith Graham from Camberley, Surrey,
with Pendle MP Andrew Stevenson

For full rules and details of how to enter, visit the website at

www.pendlewarpoetrycompetition.blogspot.co.uk

email entries to: pendlewarpoetry@gmail.com

SORLEY, Charles Hamilton – Captain, Suffolk Regiment	LOOS MEMORIAL	FRA	37
SPINDLER, Staff Nurse, Nellie - QAIMNS	LIJSSENTHOEK MILITARY CEMETERY	BEL	11
STERLING, Robert William – Lieutenant, Royal Scots Fusiliers	DICKEBUSCH NEW MILITARY CEMETERY	BEL	10
STEWART, John Ebenezer, MC – Major, 8th Bn Border Regiment	TYNE COT MEMORIAL	BEL	15
STREETS, John William – Sergeant, York & Lancashire Regiment,	EUSTON ROAD CEMETERY	FRA	32
TEMPLER, Claude Frank Lethbridge – Captain, Gloucestershire Regiment	LOOS MEMORIAL	FRA	**37**
TENNANT - The Hon Edward Wyndham – Lieutenant, Grenadier Guards,	GUILLEMONT ROAD CEMETERY	FRA	34
THOMAS, Edward THOMAS – 2nd Lieut Royal Garrison Artillery,	AGNY MILITARY CEMETERY	FRA	19
TODD, Nicholas Herbert – Rifleman London Regiment	THIEPVAL MEMORIAL	FRA	48
TROTTER, Bernard Freeman – 2nd Lieut in (British) Leicestershire Regt	MAZINGARBE COMMUNAL CEMETERY	FRA	38
VERNEDE, Robert Ernest (R.E.) – 2nd Lieut, 3rd Bn. Rifle Brigade	LEBUCQUIERE COMMUNAL CEMETERY EXT	FRA	36
WALL, Arthur Geoffrey Nelson – 2nd Lieut, RFC	RAKE LANE CEMETERY, WALLASEY	UK	65
WALL, Leonard Comer – Lieut, Royal Field Artillery.	LIJSSENTHOEK MILITARY CEMETERY	BEL	11
WATERHOUSE, Gilbert – 2nd Lieut, Essex Regiment	SERRE ROAD CEMETERY NO. 2	FRA	44
WEST, Arthur Graeme – Captain, Oxfordshire and Bucks Light Infantry	HAC (Honourable Artillery Company) CEMETERY	FRA	35
WHITE, Bernard Charles De Boismaison - Lieut, Northumberland Fusiliers,	THIEPVAL MEMORIAL	FRA	48
WILKINSON, Eric Fitzwater MC – Captain, Leeds Rifles, West Yorkshire Regiment,	TYNE COT MEMORIAL	BEL	15
WILKINSON, Walter Lightowler – 2nd Lieut , Argyll & Sutherland Highlanders	HIGHLAND CEMETERY	FRA	35
WILSON, Theodore Percival (T.P.) Cameron – Captain, Sherwood Foresters,	ARRAS MEMORIAL	FRA	20
WINTERBOTHAM, Cyril W. – Lieut, Gloucestershire Regiment	THIEPVAL MEMORIAL	FRA	48
WORDSWORTH, Osmund BARTLE – 2nd Lieut Machine Gun Corps,	ARRAS MEMORIAL	FRA	20
YVAN, Antoine – French Poet, French Army	PERE LACHAISE CEMETERY	FRA	40
ZELLERMEYER, Robert - Austro-Hungarian Airman	PROSECCO TRIESTE	ITA	55

McCRAE, John – Lieut Colonel, Canadian Medical Corps	WIMEREUX COMMUNAL CEMETERY	FRA	51
MITCHELL, Colin – Rifleman, Rifle Brigade	POZIERES MEMORIAL	FRA	40
MITTON, Thomas Ewart – Lieutenant, Royal Engineers	DUHALLOW A.D.S.* CEMETERY	BEL	10
MORRIS, Francis St. Vincent – 2nd Lieut, No. 3 Squadron, RFC	ST. SEVER CEMETERY, ROUEN,	FRA	42
Müller-Rastatt, Gerhard Klaus – Obermatrose (pen-name Gerhard Moerner)	VLADSLO GERMAN WAR CEMETERY	BEL	16
MUNRO, Hector Hugh ('Saki') – Lance Sgt, Royal Fusiliers	THIEPVAL MEMORIAL	FRA	48
OWEN, Wilfred Salter, MC – Lieutenant, Manchester Regiment	ORS VILLAGE COMMUNAL CEMETERY	FRA	39
OXLAND, Nowell – Lieut 6th Border Regiment	GREEN HILL CEMETERY, SULVA BAY	TUR	55
PARRY, Harold – 2nd Lieut, King's Royal Rifle Corps	VLAMERTINGHE MILITARY CEMETERY	BEL	17
PEGUY, Charles – Lieutenant in 276th Infantry Regiment	CHAUCONIN-NEUFMONTIERS CEMETERY	FRA	26
PEMBERTON, Vivian Telfer MC – Captain, Royal Garrison Artillery,	BELLICOURT BRITISH CEMETERY	FRA	23
PENROSE, Claude Quale Lewis, MC and Bar, - Major, Royal Garrison Artillery	ESQUELBECQ MILITARY CEMETERY	FRA	28
PHILIPPS, The Hon. Colwyn Erasmus Arnold – Captain, Royal Horse Guards	MENIN GATE MEMORIAL	BEL	14
PITT, Bernard – 2nd Lieut Border Regiment,	ARRAS MEMORIAL	FRA	20
RATCLIFFE, Alfred Victor – Lieutenant, West Yorkshire Regiment	FRICOURT NEW MILITARY CEMETERY	FRA	33
ROBERTSON, Alexander – Corporal, Sheffield Bn., York & Lancaster Reg.	THIEPVAL MEMORIAL	FRA	48
ROBINS, George Upton – Captain, 3 Bn. East Yorkshire Regiment	RAILWAY DUGOUTS (TRANSPORT FARM)	BEL	12
ROSENBERG, Isaac – Suffolk Regiment	BAILLEUL ROAD EAST CEMETERY,	FRA	22
RUB, Leslie George RUB – Private, Australian Pioneers	DICKEBUSCH NEW MILITARY CEMETERY	BEL	10
SAMUEL, Gerald George – Lieutenant, Queen's Own Royal West Kent Regt	MENIN GATE MEMORIAL	BEL	14
SCANLAN, William M , MC, MM – 5th Bn, 1st Canadian Division,	BARLIN COMMUNAL CEMETERY EXT	FRA	22
SEEGER, Alan – Legionnaire (Private), French Foreign Legion	LIHONS FRENCH NATIONAL CEMETERY	FRA	36
SHAW-STEWART, Patrick – Lieut Comm, Hood Battn, Royal Naval Division,	METZ-EN-COUTURE COMMUNAL CEM'Y	FRA	39
SHORT, William Ambrose CMG – Lieut Col Royal Field Artillery	CITE BONJEAN MILITARY CEMETERY	FRA	26
SIDGWICK, Arthur Hugh – Captain, Royal Garrison Artillery	MENDINGHEM MILITARY CEMETERY	BEL	12
SIMPSON, Henry Lamont – 2nd Lieut, Lancashire Fusiliers	VIS-EN-ARTOIS MEMORIAL & CEMETERY	FRA	50
SIMPSON, John Watt – 2nd Lieut, Border Regiment	VAUX EN AMIENOIS COMMUNAL CEMETERY	FRA	49
SIORDET, Gerald Caldwell MC – 2nd Lieut, Rifle Brigade	BASRA WAR MEMORIAL	IRQ	54
SMITH, Geoffrey Bache – Lieutenant, Lancashire Fusiliers	WARLINCOURT HALTE BRITISH CEMETERY	FRA	50
SMITH, Hugh STEWART – Captain, Argyll and Sutherland Highlanders	CATERPILLAR VALLEY CEMETERY	FRA	26
SMYLIE, Robert STEWART – Lieutenant, Royal Scots Fusiliers	FLATIRON COPSE CEMETERY	FRA	33
SOLOMON, Louis B – Lieutenant, Royal Flying Corps/Royal Air Force	OUTTERSTEENE COMMUNAL CEMY EXT	FRA	40
SORGE, Reinhard - 6th Company of 69th Reserve Infantry Regiment	VERMANDOVILLERS GERMAN CEMETERY	FRA	49

FIELD, Henry Lionel – 2nd Lieut, Royal Warwickshire Regiment	SERRE ROAD CEMETERY NO. 2	FRA	44
FLEX, Walter – Leutnant, 3rd N/Schles Inf	HAUPTFRIEDHOF EISENACH	GER	55
FLOWER, Clifford – Driver in Royal Warwickshire Regiment,	ARRAS MEMORIAL	FRA	20
FRESTON, Hugh Reginald (Rex) – 3rd Royal Berkshire Regiment	BECOURT MILITARY CEMETERY	FRA	23
GRAY, John Arthur, DCM – 2nd Lieut, Royal Berkshire Regiment	SAILLY-SAILLISEL BRITISH CEMETERY	FRA	41
GRENFELL, The Hon. Gerald William – Lieutenant, Rifle Brigade, 2 Bn.	MENIN GATE MEMORIAL	BEL	**13**
GRENFELL, The Hon. Julian Henry Francis, DSO – Captain, 1st Royal Dragoons	BOULOGNE EASTERN CEMETERY	FRA	24
HALE, Sydney – Rifleman, 8th Battalion, Rifle Brigade	MENIN GATE MEMORIAL	BEL	14
HAMILTON, William Robert – 2nd Lieut, Coldstream Guards	TYNE COT MEMORIAL	BEL	15
HARDYMAN, John Hay Maitland, DSO, MC – Lieut-Col, Somerset Light Infantry.	BIENVILLERS MILITARY CEMETERY	FRA	23
HARVEY-JAMES, Arthur - (Arthur Scott Craven) Captain (Buffs) Royal East Kent Regiment	ST. PATRICK'S CEMETERY, LOOS	FRA	41
HASELDEN, Percy – Private, King's Liverpool Regiment	THIEPVAL MEMORIAL	FRA	47
HEALD, Ivan, MC – Lieut. Royal Flying Corps	CABARET-ROUGE BRITISH CEMETERY	FRA	25
HOBSON, John Collinson – Licut, Royal Scots Regiment	MENIN GATE MEMORIAL	BEL	14
HODGSON, William Noel, MC - Lieut Devonshire Regiment	DEVONSHIRE CEMETERY,	FRA	26
HORNE, Cyril Morton - Captain, King's Own Scottish Borderers,	MAZINGARBE COMMUNAL CEMETERY	FRA	38
HULME, Thomas Ernest – Honourable Artillery Company	COXYDE MILITARY CEMETERY,	BEL	9
JENKINS, Arthur Lewis – Lieut, RFC	RICHMOND CEMETERY	UK	65
JOHNSON, Donald F GOOLD – Lieut 2 Bn Manchester Regiment,	BOUZINCOURT COMMUNAL CEMETERY	FRA	23
KELLY, Frederick Septimus, DSC – Lieut Commander, RNVR	MARTINSART BRITISH CEMETERY	FRA	38
KETTLE, Thomas Michael – Lieutenant, Royal Dublin Fusiliers	THIEPVAL MEMORIAL	FRA	47
KILMER, Alfred Joyce – Sergeant, 165 US Infantry Regiment.	OISE-AISNE AMERICAN CEM'Y & MEM	FRA	39
LANGSTAFF, James MILES – Major, 76 Bn. Canadian Infantry,	VILLERS STATION CEMETERY	FRA	49
LANGTON, Hugh Gordon – 2nd Lt, London Regiment, Royal Fusiliers	POELCAPELLE BRITISH CEMETERY	BEL	12
LEDWIDGE, Francis Edward – L/Corporal, Royal Inniskilling Fusiliers,	ARTILLERY WOOD MILITARY CEMETERY	BEL	9
LEIGHTON, Rolland Aubrey – Lieut, Worcester Regiment,	LOUVENCOURT MILITARY CEMETERY	FRA	37
LEWIS, Frank C. – Flight Sub Lieut Royal Naval Air Service,	BAILLEUL COMMUNAL CEM'Y EXT NORD	FRA	22
LICHTENSTEIN, Alfred – Bavarian 2nd Infantry Kronprinz Regiment	VERMANDOVILLERS GERMAN CEMETERY	FRA	49
LITTLEJOHN, William Henry – Company Sergeant Major, Middlesex Regiment	WANCOURT BRITISH CEMETERY	FRA	50
LYON, Walter Scott Stuart – Lieutenant, Royal Scots Regiment	MENIN GATE MEMORIAL	BEL	14
MACKINTOSH, Ewart Alan – Lieutenant, Seaforth Highlanders	ORIVAL WOOD CEMETERY	FRA	39
MANN, Alexander James (Hamish) – 2nd Lieut 8th (Service) Bn. Black Watch	AUBIGNY COMMUNAL CEMETERY	FRA	21
MASEFIELD, Charles John Beech, MC – North Staffordshire Regiment	CABARET-ROUGE BRITISH CEMETERY	FRA	25

ALPHABETICAL LIST OF CASUALTIES

CASUALTY	CEMETERY	Country	PG
APOLLINAIRE, Guillaume – French Poet, French Army	PERE LACHAISE CEMETERY	FRA	40
ARBOUSSET, Jean – Sous-lieutenant 4e régiment de Génie	ESTREE-SAINT-DENIS	FRA	28
ASQUITH, The Hon. Raymond – Lieutenant, London Regiment	GUILLEMONT ROAD CEMETERY	FRA	34
BAKER, John Stephen Marcus – Private / Signaller, 7th London Regiment	VIS-EN-ARTOIS MEMORIAL & CEMETERY	FRA	50
BECKH, Robert Harold – 2nd Lieut, East Yorkshire Regiment	CABARET-ROUGE BRITISH CEMETERY	FRA	25
BERRIDGE, William Eric – 2nd Lieut, 2nd Somerset Light Infantry	HEILLY STATION CEMETERY	FRA	35
BERTRAND, Maurice – French poet	EUSTON ROAD CEMETERY	FRA	32
BLACKALL, Charles Walter – Lieut Colonel The Buffs	ARRAS MEMORIAL	FRA	20
BLISS, Francis Kennard – 2nd Lieutenant, Royal Field Artillery,	AVELUY WOOD (LANCASHIRE DUMP) C'TRY	FRA	22
BRANDON, Thomas (Tom) – Private, East Lancs Regiment	MENIN GATE MEMORIAL	BEL	13
BRAY, Horace Edgar Kingsmill Bray – 2nd Lieut, RAF	SHOTWICK (ST. MICHAEL'S) CHURCHYARD	UK	65
BROOKE, Henry Brian - Captain, Gordon Highlanders	ABERDEEN SPRING BANK CEMETERY	UK	64
BROOKE, Rupert Chawner – Sub-Lieutenant, RNVR.	SKYROS ISLAND	GRE	57
BROWN, John, MC – Lieut, 6th Seaforth Highlanders Terri .Force.	VOORMEZEELE ENCLOSURE NO. 3	BEL	17
BUTTERWORTH, George Sainton Kaye, MC - 2nd Lieut, Durham Light Infantry	THIEPVAL MEMORIAL	FRA	47
CAMPBELL, Ivar – Captain, Argyll and Sutherland Highlanders	BASRA WAR MEMORIAL	IRQ	54
CASSON, Stanley – Lieutenant Colonel, Intelligence Corps (WW2)	NEWQUAY (Fairpark) C of E CEMETERY	UK	63
CHESTERTON, Cecil Edward – Private, Highland Light Infantry	TERLINCTHUN BRITISH CEMETERY	FRA	45
COLLINS, David Geoffrey – Guardsman, Grenadier Guards	DELSAUX FARM CEMETERY	FRA	27
COULSON, Leslie A. – Sergeant, County of London Bn.	GROVE TOWN CEMETERY	FRA	33
CROMBIE, John Eugene – Captain 4th Bn. Gordon Highlanders	DUISANS BRITISH CEMETERY	FRA	27
CULL, Arthur Tulloch – Captain, Royal Flying Corps	ARRAS FLYING SERVICES MEMORIAL	FRA	19
DAY, Miles Jeffery GAME, DFC – Flight Commander, RNAS	CHATHAM NAVAL MEMORIAL	UK	64
De CANDOLE, Alexander (Alec) Corry Vully – Lieut, Wiltshire Regiment	AUBIGNY COMMUNAL CEMETERY	FRA	21
De RUYTER, Gaston – Belgian poet and pilot in 11th Escadrille	HUY / HOEI: CIMITIERE COMMUNALE	BEL	10
DEBELYANOV, Dimcho - Bulgarian Army	KOPRIVSHTITSA,	BUL	55
DENNYS, Richard Molesworth – Captain, Loyal North Lancashire Regiment	ST. SEVER CEMETERY, ROUEN,	FRA	42
DOWN, William Oliphant , MC – Captain, Royal Berkshire Regiment	HERMIES HILL BRITISH CEMETERY	FRA	35
ENGELKE, Gerrit – Gefreiter, German Army.	ETAPLES MILITARY CEMETERY	FRA	29
EVANS, Ellis Humphrey – (Hedd Wynn) Private, Royal Welch Fusiliers	ARTILLERY WOOD MILITARY CEMETERY	BEL	9
FEARNLEY, Staff Nurse, ETHEL. QAIMNS	BOULOGNE EASTERN CEMETERY	FRA	24